VETS AT LARGE

Contents

Claire Llewellyn

Story illustrated by
Steve May

Heinemann

Before Reading

Find out about

- Vets who work on farms

Tricky words

- farms
- work
- horses
- stitch
- saved
- other
- calf
- stuck

Introduce these tricky words and help the reader when they come across them later!

Text starter

Some vets work on farms. They visit farms to look after the animals. They might have to stitch a cut on a horse, or help a calf to be born. It is hard work!

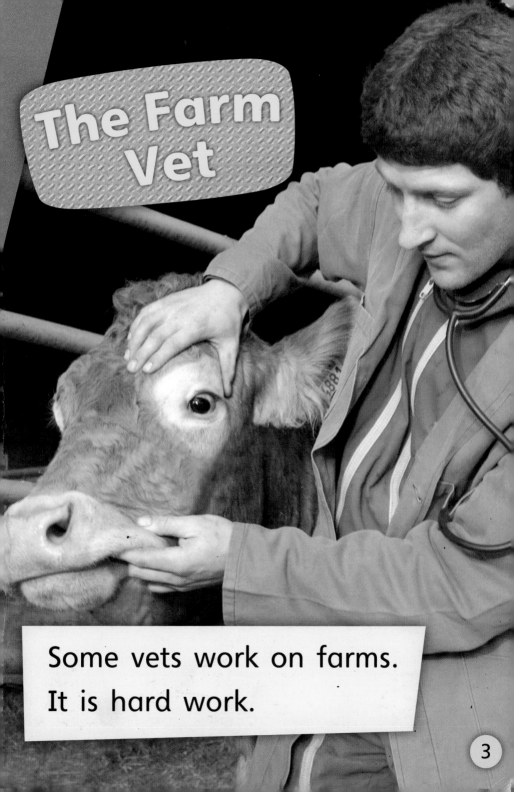

The Farm Vet

Some vets work on farms.
It is hard work.

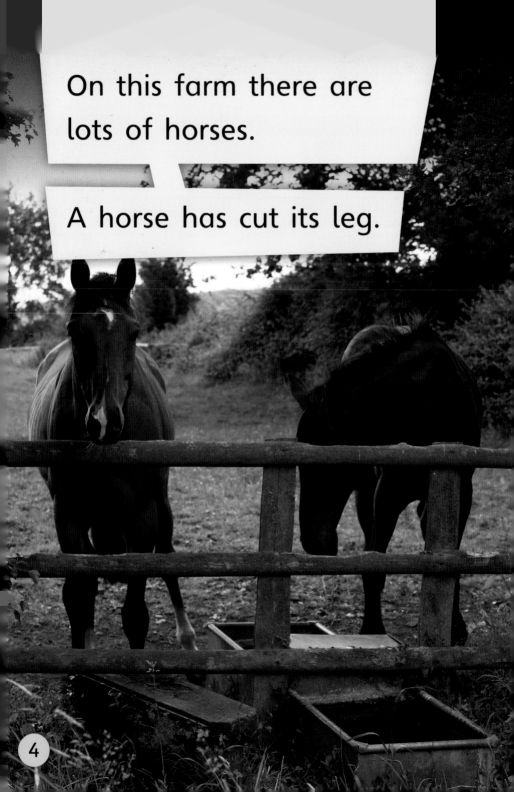

On this farm there are lots of horses.

A horse has cut its leg.

4

The vet has to stitch
the cut on its leg.

On this farm there are lots of goats.

A goat is sick.

We can make cheese from goat's milk.

The vet has to put down the sick goat.

But the vet has saved the other goats.

On this farm a cow is having a calf.

The calf is stuck.

The vet has to pull the calf out.

The vet has saved the calf!

A farm vet has to work hard to save lots of animals!

Would you like to be a vet?

Text Detective

- What work does a farm vet have to do?
- What part of a farm vet's job would you least like to do?

Word Detective

- **Phonic Focus:** Final letter sounds
  Page 3: Find a word that ends with the phoneme 'k'.
- Page 7: Find the words 'goat' and 'goats'. What is the difference between them?
- Page 8: Find a word that means 'a baby cow'.

Super Speller

Read these words:

to   cut   this

Now try to spell them!

HA! HA! HA!

Q Where do cows go for a night out?

A To the moo-vies!

Before Reading

In this story

 Jed

 Jed's mum

 The goat

Tricky words

- note
- garden
- tied
- untied
- carrots
- oats
- where
- washing

Introduce these tricky words and help the reader when they come across them later!

Story starter

Jed's mum is a vet. She looks after sick animals. Sometimes she keeps an animal overnight at her home. One day, Mum had to go out. She left a note for Jed asking him to feed the goat.

12

Jed and the Goat

Jed looked at the note.

Jed went in the garden.

The goat was tied up.

Jed untied the goat.

Jed went to get some hay.

Jed gave the goat some hay.

But the goat didn't
eat the hay.

Jed went to get some carrots.

The goat ate some socks.

Jed gave the goat some carrots.

But the goat didn't eat the carrots.

What do you think the goat will eat next?

Jed went to get some oats.

The goat ate some pants.

Jed gave the goat some oats.

But the goat didn't eat the oats.

Jed tied the goat up.

Mum got back.

"Did the goat eat?" said Mum.

"No," said Jed.

Mum looked in the garden.

"Where is the washing?"
said Mum.

Quiz

Text Detective

- Why didn't the goat eat the hay, carrots or oats?
- What do you think Jed will say to Mum about the washing?

Word Detective

- Phonic Focus: Final letter sounds
  Page 14: Find a word that ends with the phoneme 'n'.
- Pages 14 and 15: Find two words that are opposite in meaning.
- Page 23: How many sentences are there on this page?

Super Speller

Read these words:

went   did   eat

Now try to spell them!

HA! HA! HA!

 Why do baby goats like sums?

A Because they're smart kids.

24